Cheer Our Spirits,
Make Safe the Way

*Meditations for
Advent and Christmas*

Cheer Our Spirits, Make Safe the Way

Advent and Christmas are made of lived experience. The narrative of this season is a journey of raw emotions, surprise visitations, and encounters between earthly and divine forces. The rich hymns of Advent and Christmas reflect this journey. A voice in the wilderness cries out; a young peasant woman becomes a holy mother; her carpenter husband is visited by angels; together this pilgrim couple make the journey of a lifetime; a divine child is born on a holy night; heaven and nature sing. We travel along, moving from fear and uncertainty to hope and joy; from lowliness and rejection to hospitality and royal homage. We move from the shadows toward the centering light. The entire time, we are singing along.

The title of this book comes from the Advent hymn "O Come, O Come, Emmanuel." The season's centerpiece—Jesus Christ, whose

Cheer Our Spirits, Make Safe the Way

*Meditations for
Advent and Christmas*

Francisco J. García, Jr.

FORWARD MOVEMENT
Cincinnati, Ohio

MOREHOUSE PUBLISHING
New York, Harrisburg, Denver

Library of Congress Cataloging-in-Publication Data

García, Francisco (Francisco J.)
  Cheer our spirits, make safe the way : meditations for
Advent and Christmas / Francisco García.
     p. cm.
  ISBN 978-0-88028-337-3
  1. Advent—Meditations. 2. Christmas—Meditations. I.
Title.
  BV40.G36 2012
  242'.33—dc23
                          2012031127

Cover design: Albonetti Design

Scripture and Psalm quotations are from the New Revised
Standard Version Bible, copyrighted © 1989 by the
Division of Christian Education of the National Council
of Churches of Christ in the USA and used by permission.

Printed in the United States of America

Morehouse Publishing
NEW YORK · HARRISBURG · DENVER

Forward Movement
412 Sycamore Street
Cincinnati, Ohio 45202-4195
800-543-1813   www.forwardmovement.org

name means *God helps* or *God saves*—is God's supreme revelation of love in the world. He is our Emmanuel, our *God with us*. As the angel tells Joseph, Jesus will "save his people from their sins" (Matthew 1:21). Christ will simultaneously be the *God helps* and the *God with us*. This salvation will *make safe the way*, offering us nothing less than a total liberation of mind, body, and spirit. This salvation will *cheer our spirits*—it is the joy of the season. And what better way to rejoice than to sing?

Beyond waiting and longing, Advent invites us to journey and sing along with Mary and Joseph as they answer God's call. To follow the star to Bethlehem and welcome the holy child in a manger. Christmas comes, beckoning us to live into the joy and proclaim it with our very lives. The journey and nature of the Christian life is revealed, and it cannot exist without song.

This book of meditations will go from Advent to Christmas from the vantage point of journey, guided each day by the hymns of the season. Some you will know intimately, while others may be completely new to you. The Latino/a religious and cultural traditions of the season will also run throughout, with a focus on

Las Posadas, a festive nine-day prayer reenactment of the Bethlehem journey. This is a product of who I am. A Mexican American, I grew up in the physical, social, and religious borderlands of California and Mexico. I came to The Episcopal Church as a young adult. I'm a labor organizer turned seminarian, pursuing a call to the priesthood. I'm a grateful husband and father. I share these meditations from my place of culture and faith.

It is my hope and prayer that each selection will offer something to you, the reader, that draws you into the journey and joy of the season. I now invite you to join in and sing along the Advent and Christmas journey.

Paz y Bendiciones,
Francisco J. García, Jr.

❧

This booklet was written for use in Advent 2012.
To pray with this booklet in future years,
when Advent may begin earlier than December 2,
please see p. 115.

God With Us

*O come, thou Dayspring, come and cheer
our spirits by thine advent here;
disperse the gloomy clouds of night,
and death's dark shadows put to flight.*

*O come, thou Key of David, come,
and open wide our heavenly home;
make safe the way that leads on high,
and close the path to misery.*

> — *O Come, O Come, Emmanuel*
> Ninth Century, from the Latin

"O come, O come, Emmanuel" is the quintessential theme song for Advent. In it we find words of hope and longing, and the simple majesty of plainsong. The entire song evokes both the imagery and intensity of Advent, our season of Christian preparation. Before we can celebrate the joyful arrival of the Christ Child, we need to anticipate the Christ Child and prepare our whole selves for this encounter with the divine.

As we wait, Advent turns our attention to Mary, who with grace and humility carried the Christ Child. I think about Mary's humanness, and most of all, her pregnancy. As a father, I can't help but draw a comparison between awaiting the Christ Child and preparing for the arrival of my two daughters. This makes the journey real for me, as I imagine what Mary had to do to prepare for this child.

Preparing for a child requires both internal and external work, body and soul work. In my preparation, I had some major external work to do—I had to make sure that our house was ready to welcome our new arrival—and my wife had to take care of herself physically. But more importantly, we had to do serious internal work, both individually and as a couple. We had to set aside our fears and prepare for our weary and anxious selves to catch up to our forthcoming, joyful reality. We had to make a lifelong commitment of spirit and intention. We had to open wide our hearts and our home.

Welcoming the Christ Child is no different—before we can relish in the presence of God dwelling with us, we need to do the necessary exterior and interior work, personally and as a faith community.

Advent is a time to draw us into greater relationship and acceptance of our Emmanuel—*God with us*. What work will you do this Advent to open wide your home, to prepare for the arrival of the Christ Child?

> *Make me to know your ways, O LORD;*
> *teach me your paths.*
>
> — Psalm 25:4

Blessing Is All Around!

Once he came in blessing,
all our ills redressing;
came in likeness lowly,
Son of God most holy;
bore the cross to save us,
hope and freedom gave us.

Still he comes within us,
still his voice would win us
from the sins that hurt us;
would to Truth convert us...

— *Once He Came in Blessing*
Johann Roh (c. 1487-1547)

In the Latina/o culture, blessing is a big deal. Growing up, I was brought up to see the blessings that surrounded me and my family. As a child, after I'd said my prayers, my mom would send me to bed with a blessing for a good night's rest. Whenever I would leave my *abuelita's* (grandmother's) house, she would tell me, "*Dios te bendiga, mijito*" ("God bless you, my little one"). In my family and in many Latina/o households, the women are the vessels of God's blessing, and thus bestowers and distributors of this blessing to their families. To this day, even though I am grown and have two children of my own, whenever I travel somewhere distant or am undertaking a major project, my mother will sit me down, lay hands on me, and say a prayer of blessing.

As the hymn above suggests, Advent begins with such a spirit of blessing, where Christ enters into the world as blessing, and comes in blessing still, within us and all around us. The coming Christ Child beckons us toward an abundant, grace-filled blessing, where hope and freedom reign, and sin and illness meet their match. It is a transformative message, enacted very simply in ordinary life.

Accepting this Advent message means preparing for and being open to the arrival of blessing at any and all moments, and then bearing witness to it in our daily lives. Now that I am a father, I try to pass on the blessing to my children each day, as I received it. In so doing, the blessing returns, and I can't help but pass it on to others as I go about my day. Therein lies the meaning of Christ's blessed arrival, and the very purpose of the Christian life: to claim and pass on God's blessing to all people.

Advent gives us a chance to reengage in the blessedness of all of life's moments. During this season, I invite you to ask yourself—how can I be a vessel of blessing?

They will receive
blessing from the Lord,
and vindication from
the God of their salvation.

— Psalm 24:5

Finding Our Highway

There's a voice in the wilderness crying,
a call from the ways untrod:
Prepare in the desert a highway,
a highway for our God!

— *There's a Voice in the Wilderness Crying*
James Lewis Milligan (1876-1961)

One of the first signs for us of Christ's birth is the work and proclamations of John the Baptist, the voice heard crying in the wilderness. John's steadfast and alternative setting for ministry prepares believers to follow in the way that will be made known through Christ. John is the first to call the faithful to *metanoia*, a total transformation and turning away from self-absorbed ways.

Can you think of someone in your life who, like John, is a trailblazer of sorts? Someone who has paved the way for your transformation, pushed you beyond your limits? For me it was my oldest sister. She was the first in our entire extended family—a working-class family born of Mexican immigrants—to attend college. She was disciplined, driven, and motivated to achieve and bring others along in the process. There were times when her drivenness bothered me, because it made me see my faults and where I was not working hard enough to realize my potential. John the Baptist, in his effort to prepare the way for Christ, also bothered people a bit, calling them to live renewed lives and to serve others. My sister was my John the Baptist. It was through her, in seeing her achieve against the odds and knowing her belief in my ability, that I felt resolute in making my way as well. She prepared me for the journey that lay ahead. John prepared the faithful for the bumpy road that would lead them to Jesus, and to the joys and trials of attempting discipleship.

At first I thought following in my sister's path meant that I needed to do exactly as she did. She went into business and later teaching; so should I. As I embarked on that journey I saw that this was not my path. My sister's path gave me the foundation to create my own authentic way, drawing strength and encouragement from her example. John calls us out to the wilderness not to remain with him, but to direct us to our own intended highway to the Christ Child and to follow Christ's example of servanthood in the world. John the Baptist calls us to transformation, and points us in a radical new direction.

Where is your highway headed this Advent?

Almighty God, by whose providence your servant John the Baptist was wonderfully born, and sent to prepare the way of your Son our Savior by preaching repentance: Make us so to follow his teaching and holy life, that we may truly repent according to his preaching. Amen.

— Collect for the Nativity of Saint John the Baptist, *The Book of Common Prayer*, p. 241

Sharing Welcome and Love

People, look east. The time is near
of the crowning of the year.
Make your house fair as you are able,
trim the hearth and set the table.
People, look east and sing today:
Love, the guest, is on the way.

— People, Look East *
Eleanor Farjeon (1881-1965)

A number of years ago, early in my process of discerning a call to ordained ministry, I made my first solo retreat at Mount Calvary in Santa Barbara, California, a community of Episcopal/Anglican monastic brothers in the Benedictine tradition, recommended to me by my spiritual director. I was excited to attend, especially because I worked an intense and stressful job.

I had had little direct experience with monasticism, except that I had been drawn to the writings of Roman Catholic monk and writer Thomas Merton, but when I arrived at the center, I immediately felt the welcoming presence of the community and immersed myself in the rhythm of praying five times a day. Through spending quiet time in prayer and reading and by engaging in individual and group conversations with the monks, I learned of their personal vows and their collective ministry to serve and welcome all seekers and travelers as if they were Christ. I experienced this welcome as an incredible, tangible act of love and a true ministry of presence; communities like Mount Calvary have long embraced this in their daily practice.

As today's hymn powerfully reminds us, Christ *is* Love, and is our guest. Love and hospitality are intertwined, are central to the Christian life and faith, and they are most palpable in concrete actions. Thus, we must prepare to receive Christ from a place of sincere, all-embracing hospitality. We are called to look East, welcoming the holy family that is bearing Christ, and welcoming and embracing their love. We are called to share their love boldly and graciously in our own homes and houses of worship. We are challenged to create welcoming spaces for all of God's people, regardless of life circumstance, theological belief, appearance, or language. We must welcome people in suits and people in sandals; those who look just like us, and those who look nothing like us. If Christ is the guest, and we are all made in God's image, then all people are guests to be welcomed.

If we think of every person whom we encounter on our journey as Christ, how then might we act toward them? How might we welcome them into our sacred spaces and places this Advent?

Welcome one another, therefore,
just as Christ has welcomed you,
for the glory of God.

— Romans 15:7

Saint Nicholas, Compassionate Gift-Giver

Confessor of thy Son who died
Is Nicholas, our saintly guide,
Whose feast with double joy is filled,
If hearts be with thy grace instilled.

— *Almighty God of Boundless Love* *
P.A. Sutherland (1943-   )

About a dozen years ago, while I was living and studying in Merida, Yucatan, in the southeast region of Mexico, I was startled by something I observed on the main thoroughfare of the city. It was December, and the city was decorated beautifully with lights, nativity scenes, and other things. Among those other things were

---

* From *Hymns in Honour of Certain Saints: Under Whose Blessed Patronage some Fraternal Bodies Exist*, published by Paul Sutherland © 2000. No objection to free use. Reproduced by permission.

gigantic Santa Clauses hanging from light poles. In a city where the majority of the working population is of indigenous Mayan descent, with only a percentage of the population of mixed Spanish Indian heritage, the image of an "American" Santa was quite shocking, about the most foreign, unrelated image to the birth of the Christ Child that one could imagine. This Santa Claus—the one we see in most movies, books, and shopping malls—is also far from the original "Saint Nick." Today, on his feast day, is a good day to ponder the original man, why he would have been a better fit in Merida, and why he makes an excellent Advent saint.

Saint Nicholas, the person from whom Santa originated, was a bishop in the region that is now the modern-day southern coast of Turkey, a Greek region at the time. He lived in the fourth century, and was known to be a generous person. He became known as a protector and advocate for all those who were in trouble or need, especially sailors, children, and the poor. In the East he became known as a miracle-worker, and in the West as a gift-giver and protector of children. From this emerged the idea of Santa Claus in the West, which became commercialized only in the last hundred years with the help of popular magazine illustrations and advertisements. Very quickly, the consumption fueled by Santa Claus replaced the compassion shown by Saint Nicholas. The real Saint Nick was rooted in the message of the Christ Child born at Bethlehem, and gave gifts and other forms of support to children and other voiceless groups that needed them.

While Santa Claus is likely here to stay, we can bring him back to his Saint Nicholas roots through our actions and deeds. This would be a true gift during Advent!

Almighty God, in your love you gave your servant Nicholas of Myra a perpetual name for deeds of kindness both on land and sea: Grant, we pray, that your Church may never cease to work for the happiness of children, the safety of sailors, the relief of the poor, and the help of those tossed by tempests of doubt or grief. Amen.

— Collect for the Feast of Saint Nicholas, *Lesser Feasts and Fasts 2006*, p. 97

Finding Comfort in Advent's Peace

Comfort, comfort ye my people,
speak ye peace, thus saith our God;
comfort those who sit in darkness,
mourning 'neath their sorrows' load.

— *Comfort, Comfort Ye My People*
Johann G. Olearius (1611-1684)

For many people, Christmas is just too much to bear. For people who have lost a loved one, the holiday season is a reminder of their physical absence. For those struggling in any number of ways—addiction, depression, poverty, or unemployment—the joy and pomp of the season can seem trivial and empty, both in the religious and consumer aspects of the holiday. At times expectations are too high or unrealized, and stress is at a peak over finances or strained relationships. It is no wonder that people get the holiday blues at times like these. It can be overwhelming, and we as the church, in general, seem ill-equipped to ease the pain; or when we try, sometimes it's not enough. The commercial context of Christmas in the United States is powerful and unrelenting.

Advent, in contrast to Christmas, is intended as a subdued, contemplative journey. It can be the antidote to the consumer-drenched culture of packed malls, traffic jams, and electrified reindeer on front lawns. From the underbelly of secular Christmas, community, intentionality, depth, and meaning can be found. Instead of gifts and money, Advent can be a time of counter-cultural activity of the Spirit. Our gifts can be our *presence* and time with people rather than *presents*. In the quietude of Advent, we can attempt to make peace with our struggles, the demons that perhaps possess us and prevent us from thoroughly accepting the true joy that comes with Christmas. Beneath all the glitter, there is simple, peaceful joy that comes with the message of Christ, and this can be recovered at Advent.

In Advent, we can seek and find comfort; comfort that we might not find once Christmas arrives. The onslaught of Christmas may always be too great for some. But in the weeks that precede it, a tiny seed of comfort can be planted in our souls. The birth of Christ can bring comfort to us because of the promise of peace and the life that Christ will lead to model humanity for all.

Where in your life are you seeking peace or comfort this Advent?

> *Wait for the LORD;*
> *be strong,*
> *and let your heart take courage;*
> *wait for the LORD.*

— Psalm 27:14

Energized and Amazed

Lift up your voice with strength.
Lift it up, don't be afraid.
Behold your God.
Arise, and shine,
for the light of the world is come.
Behold your God!

— *Behold Your God*
African American Spiritual,
Words from Isaiah 40:9; 60:1

During the Babylonian exile, the people of Israel are in deep collective despair. They have been rooted out of their homeland—dismissed, disgraced, and deported, made subject to military power. They fear losing their livelihood, and their sense of religious and cultural identity as a people. In the midst of this despair, God calls a prophet to speak words of comfort and encouragement: *Lift up your voice...don't be afraid...Behold your God!*

While the traditional focus on Advent has been penitence, the story of exile and the cause of speaking to justice issues, of speaking one's truth of experience and faith, is often overlooked. In communities that have experienced the pain of exile or other forms of marginalization, acknowledging the experience and finding a way out is an essential part of the journey. This is how songs and words like "Behold Your God" arise in the collective African American experience and tradition. Uplifting songs speak to the strength of the community, providing encouragement for the journey that follows. Songs like these give communities that have struggled meaning and purpose in their effort at recovering their dignity. Prophetic words give communities a way of speaking their truth and achieving well-being by providing hope.

So much of the music and feeling of Advent involves extensive reference to the Hebrew Bible, and in particular the book of Isaiah. Christ comes not to replace the old understandings of these passages but to affirm them and give them further revelation to a greater number of people; there need be no effort to discount the experiences of the Jewish people—either biblically or today—in order for Christian communities to find deep meaning in these words and to proclaim them through song.

Hebrew Bible scholar Walter Brueggemann, in *The Prophetic Imagination* (Minneapolis: Augsburg Fortress, 2001), speaks of the *prophetic energizing* and *amazement* that is created through the work of the prophets. Through this process, we are all able to find ways to lift up our voices to God, knowing that God will receive our petitions, carry us through the struggles of life, and bring us to places of joy.

During Advent, as we prepare to receive Christ, may we be strengthened by the words that proclaim the enduring power of God for all people, and may we allow the prophetic energizing and amazement to enter in.

> *He will feed his flock like a shepherd;*
> *he will gather the lambs in his arms,*
> *and carry them in his bosom,*
> *and gently lead the mother sheep.*

— Isaiah 40:11

Yearning for Rest

Come, thou long-expected Jesus,
born to set thy people free;
from our fears and sins release us,
let us find our rest in thee.

— *Come, Thou Long-Expected Jesus*
Charles Wesley (1707-1788)

After graduate school, during my first year of full-time work as a union organizer, I was physically and emotionally restless. I completely identified with the work both politically and socially; I wholeheartedly believed in what I was doing, and that I was making a difference in people's lives. I was so committed that I was regularly working sixty to seventy hours each week. But in the process, I was quickly fading. I soon longed for escape on a weekly basis, and then daily. Around the same time, I had started going to church again after searching for a faith community, and I was being transformed internally.

I found myself using my lunch breaks to go to the noon eucharist at my church, which was miles away. I was drawn to ministry and felt like being at church often. My restlessness was a spiritual signal. I went to speak to a priest at my church, and she told me that "God was messing with me," and to "pay attention." Over a period of several months, I found myself growing increasingly centered in God's freedom, and I discovered the motive behind my spiritual restlessness. I began examining a potential call to the priesthood.

Our lives can be an endless cycle, a daily burden of toil with little reward. We seek meaning in many things—addictive habits, negative relationships, personal guilt, holding on to grudges. These are our "sins"—not in a moralistic or judgmental sense—but in a self-sabotaging sense. I believe that sins are the things that we do—in thought, word, or deed—that keep us from being our authentic, God-given selves; and the same goes for when we keep others from living their authentic lives. Since we are all made in God's image, when we violate either ourselves or other people, we separate from our divine origins and intentions. Jesus comes to remind us that our rest and ultimate liberation comes in returning to God, our source of life, and in Christ who is God's redeeming presence on earth.

The deep longing of Advent finds its sweet relief when we realize that the long-expected Jesus has already come and is waiting for us to find our unique call in life.

> *My soul thirsts for you,*
> *my flesh faints for you,*
> *as in a dry and weary land*
> *where there is no water.*

— Psalm 63:1

A God of Mercy and Radical Love

...that when next he comes with glory,
and the world is wrapped in fear,
with his mercy he may shield us,
and with words of love draw near.

— *Hark, a Thrilling Voice Is Sounding!*
Sixth Century, from the Latin

I recall that in high school I felt disturbed by the messages I would hear from the pulpit at the church of my upbringing. I made my first communion, was confirmed, and married and worshiped there until I eventually decided to leave, but even as a teenager, the message was too guilt-ridden, too limiting, and the God they described too micromanaging and disciplinary to speak to me.

From my mother, who taught me how to pray, I knew of an all-loving, compassionate God who sent angels to watch over us at night. This is the God that I prayed to each night, asking for my daily bread, and the one that sought to show me the way of forgiveness as a way of also receiving forgiveness. But the God I often heard about in sermons wanted to chastise me, looked at me as a helpless sinner, and didn't talk all that much about forgiveness. The God portrayed in my childhood church was wrapped up in the fear of the world.

This is not the God of Advent, who proclaims love made known through the sending of a Son. The God that sends Christ moves us from living life—as Henri Nouwen so eloquently puts it—in the "house of fear" to the "house of love" (*In the House of the Lord*, United Kingdom: Darton, Longman & Todd, 1986). Many of us live in the house of fear—where hatred, ignorance, selfishness, and greed are fomented—often held there by years of hearing punitive notions about God. However, Christ resides in the house of love, and invites us there.

Another lesson of Advent, for all time, is the mercy that Christ shows all people and his radical invitation to love. I finally walked out of my childhood church, in the middle of a sermon, as an act of love—because I could no longer hear God's word professed from a place of fear.

Living in the house of love, we will approach each relationship, each encounter with a fellow person differently. We will treat our loved ones and our not-so-loved ones with greater care and humility. We will seek the path of forgiveness and justice.

This Advent, may we await the coming of a Christ who is larger and more loving than our wildest imagination. May we move into the house of love.

Beloved, let us love one another,
because love is from God;
and everyone who loves
is born of God
and knows God.

— 1 John 4:7

Get on the Quiet Car

Speak ye to Jerusalem
of the peace that waits for them;
tell her that her sins I cover,
and her warfare now is over.

— *Comfort, Comfort Ye My People*
Johann G. Olearius (1611-1684)

I recently moved further away from where I work, so I began taking the train on the days that I go in to the office. It's about an hour's ride, and over the course of that time there are dozens of conversations taking place among co-workers who commute together and strangers who become friends because they take the same train together everyday. Wonderful conversations! People talking about their kids, commiserating about workdays, talking about vacations or weekend outings. But for those people who want a little bit of peace and quiet, it can be very noisy. There is one "quiet car" on the entire train, where no talking, cell phone use, or other loud devices are allowed. This means that the default on the train is noise, and an intentional effort has to be made for quiet on the train.

The same goes for the Advent train that we ride on to reach Christmas. The entire season can be incredibly noisy, and even violent. The noise and incessant activity can seem like a form of warfare, a place without peace. Christmas specials begin on the day after Thanksgiving, even before Advent begins. This past year some of the sales began as early as midnight, and there were reports from various regions that riots had broken out over some of the "hottest" items. One person was even trampled to death during a stampede rushing to get into a store. In this type of environment, there is little peace and quiet.

Advent presents a countercultural challenge to find intentional moments of quiet—however brief—during the season. Try driving in your car in silence rather than turning on the radio, or go for a five-minute walk at home or work. Forget trying to make it happen every day for extended periods of time. Work your way up, increasing amounts of silence, and see how it feels. Or, if you take the train to work, try riding the quiet car. Nowadays, after a day at work, I find it's the best place to be.

Are you searching for peace and quiet this Advent? What can you do today to start?

But I have calmed and quieted my soul,
like a weaned child with its mother;
my soul is like the weaned child
that is with me.

— Psalm 131:2

Día del Virgen de Guadalupe

O Virgin, the most lovely
*   of the Anahuac Valley,*
your children send you greetings
*   before the morning dawn.*
Awaken, Mother, awaken,
*   look at the day dawning,*
and receive these flowers
*   that I bring to you today.*

— *Las Mañanitas a la Virgen de Guadalupe*
Traditional (Author's translation)

The *Virgen de Guadalupe* is a Latin American version of the Mary found in Luke. Her appearance to Juan Diego in Mexico in 1531 was a way of delivering the message of Christ to a whole people. No one can verify with historical certainty the apparition of Guadalupe. Like much of our faith, it remains a mystery. However, what is certain is that for nearly five hundred years, Guadalupe has enlivened the faith of a people, remaining a core part of the *sensus fidelium*—the faith memory of the people. She is the patron saint of Mexico and of the Americas, and with good reason. She speaks to and represents all people, regardless of religious affiliation. She speaks to the humble and the lowly, promising protection and care. Because of her broad appeal, she has been called the "evangelizer of the Americas."

On December 12, during Advent, Latina/os throughout the United States and Latin America joyfully celebrate the Feast Day of the *Virgen de Guadalupe*. In some places, church members gather with mariachis (Mexican ensembles playing traditional folkloric songs and ballads) to sing "Las Mañanitas," the traditional Mexican ranchera song sung to Guadalupe. They keep vigil in the darkness just before the dawn breaks, and give thanks to this woman for shining the light of Christ to an entire people.

I have felt drawn to the Mary of Guadalupe since I was young, because my mother had prayed to her when I was ill as an infant. I was close to dying with no diagnosis or treatment. We lived in California, but my mother went to her hometown of Tijuana in desperation, seeking medical care. It was there that my mother drew from her relationship and devotion to Guadalupe, and connected with her mother to mother. She prayed to the Virgin Mary of Guadalupe for God not to take me away, since Mary already knew too well the pain of losing her own son, Jesus. I was healed. Through Guadalupe, my mother came to know Jesus.

As she has for many Latino/as, Guadalupe has remained part of my faith memory. For so many people she is also a key part of the Advent journey. May Guadalupe help us all grow closer to the coming Christ Child in our faith journey.

Do not be afraid, Mary,
for you have found favor with God.
And now, you will conceive in your womb
and bear a son, and you will name him Jesus.

— Luke 1:30-31

Enriched With Blessings

He comes, the broken heart to bind,
the bleeding soul to cure;
and with the treasures of his grace
to enrich the humble poor.

> — *Hark the Glad Sound! The Savior Comes*
> Philip Doddridge (1702-1751)

I grew up working-class in the United States. My parents were employed, but they bought clothing on lay-away, I owned one pair of shoes at a time until they were worn out, and I qualified for my school district's reduced lunch program. Still, this experience had not prepared me for the poverty that I witnessed when I traveled to rural regions of Mexico and Brazil. Here, most of the houses had no windows or doors; the roofs were thatched, the walls made of adobe, the floors were hard dirt, and hammocks served as beds. Cooking took place on a makeshift *comal* (griddle)—a piece of sheet metal placed on top of three large rocks on the floor. Yet somehow, in this place of material poverty, the people exhibited spiritual wealth. They shared what little food they had with me, a stranger. These were sacred meals, among the best I've ever had. God, through grace, had enriched the humble poor, and had also enriched me in the process.

God's work with the poor is further enriched with Jesus' Advent. Christ, from the very beginning of his arrival, makes a commitment to both material and spiritual wholeness and justice. When he says "blessed are the poor" in one scripture and "blessed are the poor in spirit" in another, these words are complementary, not contradictory; both are valid and intended. God's vision seeks blessing on all: to lift the poor out of poverty, and to raise the poor in spirit (anyone who is suffering) out of their difficult state. God's grace is freely given and is brought to greater fruition when we join God in the effort of healing hearts, souls, and bodies through acts of justice and compassion.

Dom Helder Camara, a former archbishop in Brazil, is famously known for saying that "When I give food to the poor, they call me a saint. When I ask why the poor have no food, they call me a communist." Regardless of what we're called, the gospel compels us to ask these questions and more, to make the peace of the Christ Child real by actualizing justice in his name. The Advent call is clear, decisive, and inclusive: to bind broken hearts, cure bleeding souls, and enrich the poor through acting on God's grace.

How might you act on a pressing justice or social issue this Advent?

Is not this the fast that I choose:
to loose the bonds of injustice,
to undo the thongs of the yoke,
to let the oppressed go free,
and to break every yoke?
Is it not to share your bread with the hungry,
and bring the homeless poor into your house;
when you see the naked, to cover them,
and not to hide yourself from your own kin?

— Isaiah 58:6-7

Sustainable Joy

Our hope and expectation,
O Jesus, now appear;
arise, thou Sun so longed for,
above this darkened sphere!
With hearts and hands uplifted,
we plead, O Lord, to see
the day of earth's redemption
and ever be with thee.

— *Rejoice, Rejoice Believers*
Laurentius Laurenti (1660-1722)

Christ enters the world as both God's Son and our Sun, as the coming of the dawn. Like the sunrise, the hope and expectation of the coming Christ is a daily Advent occurrence. When Christ is born, honoring his birth becomes a daily occurrence. Redemption comes when we embrace the daily majesty of life and celebrate the whole season as a marker of this reality.

As Christ calls us to our own deliverance from the woes of life, his arrival also calls for the redemption, or healing, of the earth. As beings made in God's image, we are stewards, the care-takers of all creation. This means that the joy we are preparing for during Advent is not just about people, but about the whole of the earth as we know it. As Psalm 24 says, "The earth is the LORD's and all that is in it, the world, and those who live in it."

This is a crucial point to embrace, especially during the Advent season when the commercial side of Christmas is at its most forceful and the temptation to buy lots of presents and items for our friends and family is great. While it seems fine to show our love and generosity for others through gift-giving, there is a point at which it becomes too much. And indeed, it usually is too much. Our fragile earth groans when we consume an inordinate amount of products that we cannot recycle or reuse, and when we travel all over creation to find the perfect gift. I say this because I am just as guilty as the next person of this habit!

Every year, early in Advent, my church holds an Alternative Christmas Market, a day-long event where people can purchase handmade, sustainable goods and products that are fairly traded and support local economies, or contribute to nonprofit organizations that work on a range of environmental, social justice, and pastoral care issues. It is a lively, well-attended event. Some people do their entire Christmas shopping at this event. Perhaps you can find—or start—a similar market in your community.

Preparing for Christ's arrival reminds us that the earth's redemption is wrapped up in our own. We are all God's creation!

Give us all a reverence for the earth as your own creation, that we may use its resources rightly in the service of others and to your honor and glory.

— from The Prayers of the People,
The Book of Common Prayer, p. 388

Hope and Harvest

The grain is ripe, the harvest comes!
Good seed of hope, your time is now!

— The Grain is Ripe *
Shirley Erena Murray (1931-   )

The harvest is the peak of the farming season, where the fruits of labor are gathered. The work required to get to this point is also extensive, but the harvest is the most labor intensive part of the agricultural process; even today, with the mechanization of agriculture, harvesting requires the largest and most costly machinery in addition to thousands of seasonal migrant workers who are needed to secure the harvest. Because the crops are ripe, timing is crucial.

Jesus repeatedly indicated that the work of God's kingdom, like a harvest, was to be done

---

in the here and now. He said that "the kingdom of God is among you" (Luke 17:21), and empowered disciples to begin this work immediately. Even when folks thought that their work might be through, Jesus told them that it wasn't. The work of harvest entails a lifetime of ministry and discipleship. Of course, there must be times of rest and renewal, when the fields lay fallow, as in the time of Jubilee in the Torah tradition, but the work quickly begins again.

The human project of achieving emancipation for all people is a gospel project, born in the Advent roots of harvest. This message resonates with a good portion of the Latino/a experience in the United States, as many have worked or toiled in the fields, or have parents or grandparents who did so. My grandfather was a *bracero* (a Mexican guest-worker) in the 1950s; my father picked cotton in Baja California before migrating to the North. Harvest is about working hard to accomplish the goal and being able to enjoy the fruits. This is the message of hope that begins now, even as we labor for the future.

Hope is often seen as a future-leaning message. The traditional message of Advent is one of hopeful waiting for the coming of the Christ Child. This is well and good, but the waiting of Advent does not mean passive inaction. The message of Advent is to proclaim hope now, even as we wait. It's taken some time for the grain to ripen, but the time has come for its fruit to show forth; it is time for work to be done.

He said to them, "The harvest is plentiful,
but the laborers are few;
therefore ask the Lord of the harvest
to send out laborers into his harvest.

— Luke 10:2

❦

When using this book in years
when Advent begins earlier than December 2,
please select a reading
from the Additional Meditations (p. 117)
for each day until December 16.
A reading for the Third Sunday in Advent is on p. 129.

Walking in the Cold, in the Dark

A beautiful shepherdess
was walking in the cold,
and, like a beautiful rose,
she was covered with dew.

Joseph was walking,
Mary was walking.
They walked toward Bethlehem
more by night than by day.

— Introductory prayer-song to *Las Posadas*
Traditional

Beginning on December 16, some faithful will be honoring another Christian tradition during the evening hours—with *Las Posadas*. *Las Posadas*, meaning "shelter," is the popular Latina/o religious observance and celebration through which communities reenact the journey Joseph and Mary made from Nazareth to Bethlehem, as they looked for a place to stay and give birth to the Christ Child. The *Posadas* are a form of an Advent novena, a nine-day period of prayerful preparation. *Las Posadas* give life to the Gospel of Luke where it is written that Mary placed baby Jesus in a manger because "there was no place for them in the inn" (Luke 2:7).

I recall with joy these *Posadas* that my family would engage in during the nine evenings leading up to Christmas—a prayerful retelling of the journey, imbued with song throughout. Over several evenings, we would go to different family members' houses. Someone would play Mary and Joseph seeking refuge, carrying with them statues of Mary and Joseph. The owner of the house and a family crowd (the "Chorus") would play the innkeeper and refuse to let Mary and Joseph in several times. Each side took turns singing the dialogue of the narrative.

The lyrics provided above are the first portion of the story, in the form of a prayer-song. Mary and Joseph begin their journey on foot in the cold night. As the reenactment develops, the weary travelers are refused lodging. The entire narrative continues in song, ending with rejoicing when Mary and Joseph finally receive hospitality. Once the narrative is completed, the somber mood shifts to fiesta, and it continues with food, games, more songs, and fellowship.

The *Posada* tradition has been an essential part of the Advent season for many Latina/o communities for centuries, and its staying power has been its ability to bring faith alive, addressing the major themes and lessons of Advent in a way that people can grasp and relate to. All perspectives—from Mary and Joseph, to the innkeeper, to the pilgrims and shepherds—are found and experienced in *Las Posadas*. Let us consider how we can relate not just to the coming Christ Child but to Mary and Joseph as well, and to those they encountered on their faithful journey.

What will your journey to Bethlehem be like this Advent?

> *Stir up your power, O Lord,*
> *and with great might come among us.*

— Collect for Third Sunday of Advent
The Book of Common Prayer

Pilgrimage and Rejection

They walked from tent to tent;
there was no room in the inn.
Everyone closed their door to them,
and their hearts as well.

Humble pilgrims,
Jesus, Mary, and Joseph,
I give you my soul, and with it
my heart as well.

—Introductory prayer-song to *Las Posadas*
Traditional

In this next part of the *Posada*, faithful pilgrims build upon the narrative in Luke and thicken the story-line. Here Mary and Joseph continue their pilgrimage, walking from tent to tent looking for shelter. They are thoroughly rejected and refused any kind of hospitality. Then, the narrators (the participants singing the *Posada* prayer-song) embed themselves entirely into the story, with all their heart and soul. The effect of this is the identification of the participants with the long journey and weary despair that Mary and Joseph endured.

Both themes—pilgrimage and rejection—have high relevance in the Latina/o community. As a people who have made migration pilgrimages as political exiles and economic refugees, many Latinos have faced physical, even violent, rejection. Following the U.S.-Mexican War (1846-1848), it was common, well into the 1960s, to see signs in the southwestern United States reading "No Dogs or Mexicans Allowed." Today, the increased militarization of the U.S.-Mexico border and the increased anti-immigrant sentiment seen in recent legislation indicates that the longstanding feeling of rejection is not unwarranted. Identifying with the rejection faced by Mary and Joseph gives meaning to people's harsh, lived realities, and offers hope for change to come. Christ, as the God-baby born in these conditions of rejection, gives people's experiences even more meaning.

While the themes of pilgrimage and rejection are not as prominent in traditional approaches to

Advent, in reality most of us have been rejected or treated less-than at some point in our lives, or have been on a long journey, whether physical or spiritual. Advent is about making the journey, facing the difficulties and rejections of life, but persisting in faith and finding refuge and joy along the way.

Can you imagine yourself as Mary or Joseph? How does it feel to make the pilgrimage and then be refused a place to stay? How can your greater identification with this story give greater meaning to Advent?

> *Come to me, all you that are weary*
> *and are carrying heavy burdens,*
> *and I will give you rest.*
>
> — Matthew 11:28

Mary the Star
Guides the Way

Who is that star
that guides everyone?
The Queen of Heaven,
the Virgin Mary!
We are walking,
following the footprints;
all are asking,
who is that star?

—Introductory prayer-song to *Las Posadas*
Traditional

As the reenactment of *Las Posadas* continues, we turn back to Mary. In the Latina/o tradition, we've already observed Mary as manifested on the Feast Day of the *Virgen de Guadalupe*, but we can't talk about Mary too much during Advent. After all, she is the

Christ-bearer, the one who was seen with favor in God's eyes and chosen to carry out God's mission of bringing the ultimate peacemaker, consoler, and redeemer to the earth.

In this portion of the *Posada* narrative, two more themes for Advent emerge: Mary personifying "the star of Bethlehem" that guides the participant pilgrims or lights the way, and walking in "the way"—following the footprints on the path that leads to Christ. This is the essential gospel message expressed in the *Posada* story. As Virgilio Elizondo puts it in *The Galilean Journey* (Maryknoll: Orbis Books, 2000), the *Posada* pilgrims are to "to walk as did the migrant shepherdess from Galilee, walking through the darkness of rejection toward the light that will redeem them from the idolatry of the ways of the world" (36).

Mary, the Queen of Heaven, especially in the form of Guadalupe, continues to guide the paths of communities seeking justice and mercy, which is the way of Christ. She was present in the pilgrimages and fasts of the farm workers led by union leader Cesar Chavez; she resides in the hearts of migrants trekking dangerously across the border; in men and women laboring intensely for barely enough wages to put food on the table; in student dreamers who study late into the night after working one or more jobs to pay for college. Mary continues to help countless modern-day pilgrims seek the liberating way of Christ.

Have you thought about Mary this Advent? How she can better lead you to the way of Christ?

> *Your word is a lamp to my feet*
> *and a light to my path.*
>
> — Psalm 119:105

Desperation and Fear

JOSEPH:
> *In the name of heaven*
> *I ask you for lodging,*
> *because to keep on going*
> *my beloved wife is unable.*

INNKEEPER:
> *This is not an inn;*
> *continue on your way;*
> *I can't open [the door];*
> *you may be riffraff.*

— *Las Posadas*
Traditional Mexican Carol

Following the prayer-song that narrates the overall *Posada* story is the actual dialogue, also in the form of a song, of the interaction between Mary, Joseph, and the innkeeper. In this first encounter between Joseph and the innkeeper, I think about the level of desperation that Joseph must have felt in trying to find lodging for the very pregnant Mary. Can you imagine his trepidation, first to have been told by his soon-to-be wife that she would be giving birth to God's Son? That she saw an angel? And then, at the height of Mary's pregnancy, to have to travel to Bethlehem? This is the account in Luke's Gospel. In Matthew, the story is a little different—it is Joseph who is visited in a dream by an angel and told to flee for fear of death. Either way, the setting is intended to elicit in us the deep concern that is present in the situation, even as Joseph and Mary heed God's call. Joseph speaks to the innkeeper with this burden on his shoulders. Mary, too, carries the physical and emotional weight of the pregnancy.

We must also consider the innkeeper's perspective. It was late at night, when thieves and pillagers were potentially lurking and looking to ransack villages. The innkeeper was likely afraid of the unknown and probably had legitimate reasons for refusing to let Joseph and Mary in.

Las Posadas cause people to experience a variety of emotions, sentiments, and attachments. This is a live catechesis, where people's own lives are brought into the story, to inhabit alongside the gospel story. Some people may thus identify with all the characters in the story for different reasons and at different points. This is a good thing. In inhabiting Joseph's desperation and the innkeeper's potential fear, we can better identify our own concerns and those of others.

The more we bring of our own selves into Advent, with our true emotions and concerns, and put them on God's table—or better yet, bring them on the pilgrimage to Bethlehem, laying them at the manger—the more fully we can experience God's grace and peace in the season.

Do not fear, for I am with you,
do not be afraid, for I am your God;
I will strengthen you, I will help you,
I will uphold you with my victorious right hand.

— Isaiah 41:10

Joseph Appeals to Our Humanity

JOSEPH:

> *Don't be inhumane;*
> *have charity for us*
> *that the God of heaven*
> *may repay you for it.*

INNKEEPER:

> *You may go now*
> *and don't bother us,*
> *because if I get angry*
> *I'm going to hit you.*

— Las Posadas
Traditional Mexican Carol

The innkeeper again rejects Mary and Joseph's plea for lodging, though Joseph persists in his advocacy with words that are at once a gentle chastisement of the innkeeper and an affirmation of God's promise and plan. Joseph fully believes in God's plan, about to be realized through Mary, and in the resolve and compassion that God gave him to see Mary through.

While Saint Joseph is commemorated in the church calendar in March, I'd like to make a case for making him an Advent saint. In Matthew's Gospel, we hear Joseph's side of the story. He too was visited by an angel. In a dream, an unnamed angel tells him that his betrothed Mary will give birth to a divine son, Jesus, who will "save people from their sins." Joseph, atypical for the patriarchal culture of the ancient Near East, is a faithful, anti-macho husband, a compassionate father, a working carpenter, and overall defender of his family. In responding to the angel's message and not dismissing Mary—despite the strong cultural tendency to do so—he is also deeply attentive to God's vision, just as Mary was.

When I think of Joseph, I think of my own father and the incredible pilgrimage he made, crossing the U.S.-Mexican border to seek a better life for his mother, younger brothers and sisters, and his own future family. His father had recently and suddenly passed away, leaving the family without a breadwinner. My father, only one year away from graduating from high school (a big deal for a poor family in Mexico), had to drop out to find full-time work. There was no work where he lived, so he crossed the border, found work, and began sending money back home. Despite the challenges of providing for his aging mother and own new family, my father never faltered in his commitment. Like Joseph, he appealed to God's higher power to find a way forward.

So I hereby claim Joseph as one of my Advent saints. Joseph the worker, the compassionate guardian and companion, calls us to examine our own sense of compassion and work ethic this Advent. Where in our life, family, or neighborhood is there a need for such humanity?

> *O God, who from the family of your servant David raised up Joseph to be the guardian of your incarnate Son and the spouse of his virgin mother: Give us grace to imitate his uprightness of life and his obedience to your commands; through Jesus Christ our Lord, who lives and reigns with you and the Holy Spirit, one God, for ever and ever. Amen.*

— Collect for the Feast of Saint Joseph,
The Book of Common Prayer, p. 239

Saint Thomas and the Doubting Innkeeper

MARY:
> *Asking you for lodging,*
> *kind homeowner,*
> *for only one night,*
> *is the Queen of Heaven.*

INNKEEPER:
> *If she is a queen*
> *who is asking,*
> *how is it that at night*
> *she is walking alone?*

> — *Las Posadas*
> Traditional Mexican Carol

It's very fitting that the feast day of Saint Thomas occurs during *Las Posadas*. From Thomas, a devoted but curious disciple, we learn that doubt is a real and important part of having faith. It eases our concerns over the need to be a "perfect" follower. In our humanness, we all have our doubts, at times about our faith and at times about ourselves. Thomas is a concrete, visual person; he asks for proof from his fellow disciples that they have seen Jesus, even claiming that unless he sees the mark of the nails in Jesus' hands, he would not believe. Once Thomas sees Jesus, he doesn't need to put his hands into Jesus' side, as Jesus invites him to do. Thomas knows he is in the presence of the risen, living Christ.

In the *Posada* scene, the innkeeper also exhibits some form of doubt at the claims made by the traveling pilgrims. Who is this person claiming to be the Queen of Heaven? Talk about delusions of grandeur! Here we even find a little bit of humor in the story from the innkeeper. Where is this queen's entourage? Before Jesus was doubted by Thomas, it appears that Mary, his own mother, was doubted first.

Despite the challenges our doubts create, they can be tremendously helpful, if they don't get the best of us. If channeled properly, our doubts are a good check on being blind believers of *anything*. They lead to genuine curiosity and to questions that invite us to deeper faith and reality. The innkeeper's probing, while something of a pain to the tired pilgrims, actually leads to Mary and Joseph making their case more powerfully.

This Advent, let's do a little dance with doubt, and thank Thomas and the innkeeper for challenging us to grow into our faith. We need Thomas as well as the innkeeper in our faith tradition to help us fully welcome the Christ Child.

Have you had any doubts lately? How can you bring them into your Advent journey?

> *Thomas answered him,*
> *"My Lord and my God!"*
>
> — John 20:28

The Innkeeper's Revelation

JOSEPH:
> *My wife is Mary,*
> *she is the Queen of Heaven,*
> *and she is going to be mother*
> *of the Divine Word.*

INNKEEPER:
> *Are you Joseph?*
> *Your wife is Mary?*
> *Come in, pilgrims,*
> *I did not know who you were.*

— *Las Posadas*
Traditional Mexican Carol

Here comes the moment of revelation, the point where the innkeeper realizes just who he is talking to and has a change of heart in response. Like the disciples on the road to Emmaus, where Christ is made known to them after they travel and converse with him for some time, the innkeeper finally has a breakthrough, triggered by the pilgrims' persistence in seeking shelter.

In the *Posada* reenactment, the prayer-song changes from rejection, fear, exhaustion, and doubt to revelation and conversion. This moment is the precursor to the explosion of joy, solace, and celebration soon to come. When I was a child, this was the moment in the story that I most anticipated. I remember playing one of the pilgrims outside the house and experiencing the feeling of rejection. When the innkeeper opened the door one final time and recognized Mary and Joseph, I felt relieved. He knew who we were.

Recognition is important to us as a culture and society. While we like to appear humble and say that we don't need any form of recognition, this is really a cover, a way to hide our true feelings. From our infancy, we yearn for and require attention, recognition, and affirmation, and we need it until our last breath. While the innkeeper was granting Mary and Joseph shelter, meeting a most basic requirement for survival, the meaning was much deeper than that. At a fundamental level, a spiritual transformation took place for all involved. The innkeeper was changed, acknowledging the divine presence in his midst; Mary and Joseph reached a crucial benchmark in their spiritual and geographical journey. While basic survival is an important theme in *Las Posadas*, affirmation and revelation are also key.

In my work as a labor organizer and negotiator, I often deal with the "bread and butter" issues, such as wages and benefits. But a fundamental need, just as important and often overlooked, is recognition and respect: to be valued for who you are and what you do. This *Posada* taps into this human emotion and need. Advent can be a time of revelation and clarity in our lives, and meditating and taking part in the journey and an encounter at Bethlehem can help us get there.

> *I will greatly rejoice in the LORD,*
> *my whole being shall exult in my God;*
> *for he has clothed me with*
> *the garments of salvation.*

— Isaiah 61:10a

DECEMBER 23
EIGHTH NIGHT OF *LAS POSADAS*

The Joy of Hospitality

INNKEEPER:

Come in, holy pilgrims,
accept this corner,
not of this poor house,
but of my heart.

This is a night of happiness,
of joy and rejoicing,
because we give hospitality here
to the Mother of God the Son.

— *Las Posadas*
Traditional Mexican Carol

Here we experience the joy of hospitality. After a long and treacherous journey, the exhausted pilgrims find *posada*. More than just shelter, Mary and Joseph have an experience of radical hospitality, accompanied with celebration. At last, the coming Christ Child finds a place to enter the world. In the *Posada* narrative, the welcome is ecstatic and deeply spiritual. The innkeeper and the others at the inn, now fully believers, welcome Mary, Joseph, and the accompanying pilgrim participants into the inn with a joyful song—receiving them wholeheartedly into their home. In this hospitality, there is true *metanoia* (transformation) and fellowship.

This form of hospitality is largely unknown in today's culture, where fear and notions of security reign supreme. Rich or poor, we protect our homes to keep people out. Many of our churches are gated and locked-up during the week. Lack of welcome affects every level of life, from the personal to the interpersonal, to our homes, workplaces, and places of worship.

I've been in many unwelcoming places and, unfortunately, many of them have been churches. In college, my wife and I were looking for a faith community to call home. Having grown up in different Christian traditions—she Southern Baptist and I Roman Catholic—we were searching for something that had the elements we liked from each of our traditions. Over a period of two years, we went to dozens of churches across denominations—including

Episcopal—and never quite felt welcomed. If we had been in our own *Posada* reenactment, we never got to the part where the innkeeper says "Come in, holy pilgrims." It took several years and a move across town for us to finally find our place in an Episcopal church in Pasadena, California. When we did, there was no question that it was home.

What if we took this joyous message seriously and led radically welcoming lives, everywhere we went? How might our churches and communities look different? Would we tolerate things like poverty and exclusion taking place right outside our doorsteps?

This Advent, let us pray for our hearts to be converted like the innkeeper's, to welcome the holy pilgrims who cross our paths every day. This is a sure way to make room for the Christ Child in the world.

Let mutual love continue.
Do not neglect to show hospitality to strangers,
for by doing that some have
entertained angels without knowing it.

— Hebrews 13:1-2

Let Us Sing

Let us sing, let us sing,
Merry Christmas Eve,
Merry Christmas Eve.
You are the hope, you the charity,
you all consolation for humanity.

—Cantemos, Cantemos
Traditional Mexican Carol

For many Latino/a families, this is the most important evening of the entire Advent and Christmas season. This is the night of the final *Posada*, with the biggest fiesta of the season to follow. Traditionally, this last *Posada* ends in people going to *la Misa de Gallo* (Midnight Mass), but this varies.

During the eight days leading up to this night, the *Posada* novena, while ending in food, fellowship, and song each night, still carries with it a more somber tone, or at least one of anticipation. On those days we are still waiting for the Christ Child, and still on the journey to receive *posada*. The purpose of doing this for nine days, after all, as a form of prayer and penitence, is to drive the point home. Participants have now experienced, for eight evenings, the long journey from Nazareth to Bethlehem and repeated rejection. All of this changes on *Noche Buena* (the Good Night), when pilgrims celebrate the completion of *Las Posadas*.

Noche Buena has always been Christmas for me. This is the night when my family would have traditional foods (tamales, Mexican hot chocolate, hominy soup), music, and games. We would usually gather at my grandparents' house for this evening, and all the kids would get to stay up until midnight to open presents.

While *Noche Buena* varies in different Latina/o countries and cultures, the common denominator is the importance placed on this evening. It is a time to be gathered with close family and friends, to mark the evening that Christ came into the world for the cause of humanity. While nowadays many families and churches do not observe the nine evenings of *Las Posadas*, many do gather and celebrate in churches and homes on Christmas Eve, and engage in many of the same rituals of songs, food, and games that have characterized *Las Posadas* for centuries. Generations of Latino/a families have continued the tradition of the final *Posada* and have received a deeper appreciation for the meaning of the Advent and Christmas season because of its continuation.

The *Noche Buena* tradition, a festive welcoming of Christ, is a gift to be shared with all people and continued for generations to come.

But the angel said to them,
"Do not be afraid; for see—
I am bringing you good news
of great joy for all the people:
to you is born this day
in the city of David
a Savior, who is the Messiah,
the Lord.

— Luke 2:10-11

Joy to the World!

Joy to the world! the Lord is come:
let earth receive her King;
let every heart prepare him room,
and heaven and nature sing,
and heaven and nature sing,
and heaven, and heaven, and nature sing.

— *Joy to the World*
Isaac Watts (1674-1748)

Can you imagine just how many people in how many places—choirs, parishioners, and others throughout the world—are singing this song on Christmas Day? It's like a global flash mob proclaiming "Joy to the World!" Christmas Day is the day to proclaim the sheer joy of the season, the happiness that we feel in celebrating the birth of Jesus—redeemer, savior, and liberator; friend, brother, and chief pastor—he who brings us closer to the kingdom of God. In our Episcopal tradition, we've been withholding the joy for so long during Advent, trying to focus on the waiting, trying to prepare ourselves, all while the consumer world has been celebrating secular "Christmas" in shopping malls and on radio stations for weeks. Finally, we can welcome the Christ Child that we've been waiting for by taking a breather and letting loose, right?

Yes, we can, but we have not been doing our Advent spiritual exercises just to party, eat, open presents, drink eggnog, and pass out. Why are we rejoicing, and what do we do with all this newfound joy? Key words in this popular hymn we sing and pray today can actually point us in the right direction.

First, there are the references of Jesus as King. These references point to the expectation that he was the Messiah, the "anointed one." In ancient Hebrew tradition, earthly kings, like King David, were anointed with oil as a symbol of their reign. But Jesus rarely spoke of himself as a king—he spoke most frequently about the kingdom or reign of God, or the *basilea* in Greek. *Basilea* is neither a kingdom on the earth or in some heaven beyond, but something all-encompassing that transcends both understandings. It is creating the material and spiritual conditions on earth and in people so lasting peace, justice, wholeness, mercy, joy, and compassion reign.

This is why Christ was born, and what he came to teach and build. This is the kingdom of God in our midst, always within reach, yet so far away because we push it away. Christmas Day is but a benchmark, a beginning to draw forth God's reign, a day to prepare room in our hearts, to let heaven and nature sing.

> *O God, you have caused this holy night to shine with the brightness of the true Light: Grant that we, who have known the mystery of that Light on earth, may also enjoy him perfectly in heaven; where with you and the Holy Spirit he lives and reigns, one God, in glory everlasting. Amen.*

— A Collect for the Nativity of Our Lord,
The Book of Common Prayer, p. 212

Saint Stephen,
Deacon and Martyr

O may we keep and ponder in our mind
God's wondrous love in saving lost mankind;
trace we the Babe, who hath retrieved our loss,
from his poor manger to his bitter cross;
treading his steps, assisted by his grace,
till our first heavenly state again takes place.

—*Christians, Awake! Salute the Happy Morn*
John Byrom (1692-1763)

Stephen, deacon and martyr, was "a man full
of faith and the Holy Spirit," according to the
account in Acts 6:5. From our limited knowledge
of him in the Scriptures, we know that Stephen
was among the first and most active deacons and
a great orator. This is all well and good, but why
do we observe his feast day during the twelve
days of Christmas? As a deacon, he exhibited
tremendous generosity and was respected by his

peers. So much so, that his detractors did not like what he did or said.

Stephen's generosity of spirit, his commitment to action and compassion, are themes that run all through Christmas. In Acts, Stephen and the other deacons were engaged in the practical and economic as well as spiritual needs of the community. They were lifted up in ministry to provide alms and pastoral support to the widows of the community. This is the reality and complexity of ministry, where spiritual, social, and physical concerns are completely intertwined. We see this play out in end-of-life matters, when people often go into retreat-like, deeply inward states, prior to leaving their physical bodies.

The inheritors of Stephen are those often nameless people who are working in these complex realities of ministry and vocation, working to achieve healing and wholeness in their communities. They are the unsung leaders at the grassroots level. They are deacons and chaplains, social workers, teachers, mental health workers, nurses, housing rights advocates, community organizers, volunteers, and many others. In this effort, because they are not content with things as they are, they often challenge the limiting structures of authority, as Stephen did in his last sermon. Stephen presents an ancient model of Christian service that is still valid and much needed.

Stephen followed the way of Christ—"from his poor manger to his bitter cross"—and literally gave his life to this effort. Scripture tells us that he did this with grace through the very end. Today, we honor Saint Stephen by recommitting as individuals and as faith communities to the work that he did. We can seek the life of Christ in our daily interactions and decisions, regardless of our occupations, and we will be assisted by grace in the process.

While they were stoning Stephen, he prayed,
"Lord Jesus, receive my spirit."

— Acts 7:59

Saint John,
Apostle and Evangelist

Love came down at Christmas,
love all lovely, love divine;
love was born at Christmas:
star and angels gave the sign.

Love shall be our token;
love shall be yours and love be mine,
love to God and to all men,
love for plea and gift and sign.

— *Love Came Down At Christmas*
Christina Rossetti (1830-1894)

This has to be one of my new favorite songs of the Christmas season, and a perfect fit for the Feast Day of Saint John. While so much of the Christmas season is focused on the Gospels of Luke and Matthew, John takes a completely different angle. John brings in the elements of mystery, eternity, and mysticism to the season, and is the basis for our incarnational thinking. From John we hear of Jesus as the *logos*—the Word of God made flesh that lived among us. And this Word made flesh was God's manifestation of love for the world.

The Jesus found in John repeatedly speaks of and demonstrates love to his disciples and friends, and more importantly, to those whom society says he should not be close to, should not touch, and definitely should *not* love. Just think of the Samaritan woman at the well, Jesus healing the blind man, Jesus and Lazarus, and Jesus as the Good Shepherd. His was a deep love of divine origins, an active, constant, caring, servant love, readily given and made available to us through his birth and his life example.

We share in this love when we embody it in all of our life. But what about love for *the other*? The greatest indication of love is when you demonstrate concern for someone that you have no reason to love, or actually might have better "reason" to hate. Think of the reconciliation work of restorative justice. I heard a story of a young man who shot and killed another teenage boy indiscriminately, without any cause or motive. Both boys were raised by single fathers, and both fathers were terrified and in deep despair over the incident. The father of the murdered son, rather than seek vengeance, intentionally sought the other father and together they began speaking to high school youth in their area about the tragedy and how to promote peace and dialogue in the schools. Their story has so moved people that the fathers began speaking about it across the country. The boy who committed the crime, now serving a life sentence, has been changed in the process as well. He was forgiven by the other father, has asked for forgiveness, and has accepted the responsibility and consequences for his actions.

In the spirit of John's Gospel and the Jesus he describes, may we carry God's token of love for us everywhere we go!

Shed upon your Church, O Lord, the brightness of your light, that we, being illumined by the teaching of your apostle and evangelist John, may so walk in the light of your truth.

— Collect for Saint John, Apostle and Evangelist, *The Book of Common Prayer,* p. 238

Holy Innocents

Silent night, holy night,
Son of God, love's pure light
radiant beams from thy holy face,
with the dawn of redeeming grace,
Jesus, Lord at thy birth.
Jesus, Lord at thy birth.

— *Silent Night*
Joseph Mohr (1792-1848);
translated by
John Freeman Young (1820-1885)

The rich imagery described in this song, along with its simple musical beauty, makes it a Christmas favorite. It creates the setting for us to sit and imagine the silence of the night when Christ was born and to search for the light that brings radiance to the night sky. But nighttime for so many people also means danger, as we see in the gospel story where King Herod seeks to eliminate baby Jesus. While Herod fails to find Jesus, he terrorizes the region's families by killing their children, reminding us of the threat that Jesus already brought to the empire.

But the night described in this song is different. This night remains holy. It's as if time stops, the cosmic forces are at a standstill, as the universe dwells in quiet next to the sleeping Christ Child. This is very sentimental, but in its simplicity it reaches us at a core, gut level. Our desire for peace, tranquility, and joy is so great, and here it comes, in the form of a divine child.

For the many of us who now live in large urban areas, finding this kind of evening silence is hard to come by. Where I live, sadly I cannot even see stars on most nights because it is either too smoggy or too bright with artificial light. I often go back to my experiences of living and studying abroad in the Yucatan Peninsula of Mexico, because it is a time in my life that led to a major shift in my thinking, spirituality, and identity. It took me out of my comfort zone and regular life. During a week-long stay in a village on the outskirts of the city, the electricity was minimal. There were only a few lights in the town square, and most of the homes had no installed lighting—you had to bring your own lanterns or flashlights. So when dusk hit, and the evening came on, it got incredibly dark. Pitch black, in fact. One night, when this darkness fell, I went outside to get some fresh air before going to bed. As I walked further onto the dirt road, I looked up and saw a sky loaded with stars. Then I looked down, and began to see shiny bright lights floating in the air—as a city boy, it was the first time that I had seen fireflies. The setting was serene, majestic, much like a silent, holy night in Bethlehem.

We can repeat the feeling and setting of that fateful night throughout Christmastide and beyond, by finding ways to enjoy silent nights in our lives.

O Lord, our Sovereign,
how majestic is your name in all the earth!
You have set your glory above the heavens.

— Psalm 8:1

God Abides in the Stillness

O holy Child of Bethlehem,
descend to us, we pray;
cast out our sin and enter in,
be born in us today.
We hear the Christmas angels
the great glad tidings tell;
O come to us, abide with us,
our Lord Emmanuel!

— *O Little Town of Bethlehem*
Philips Brooks (1835-1893)

I once read about an ancient Christmas tradition based in practicality: that one's house needed to be completely cleaned up, all household and labor-related matters finished, and that any items that had been borrowed needed to be returned before nightfall on Christmas Eve. This was, of course to prepare for celebrating the coming of the Christ Child and the entire twelve days of Christmastide, which was seen to be a time of sacred or holy leisure—a sort of extended sabbath—when no new work or tasks would be initiated. This is what I think it means for us to ask for Christ to "descend to us…be born in us… abide with us."

I absolutely love the notion of sacred leisure, and think that it is something worth recovering in our busy social calendars and lives, including our church calendars. Once the fanfare of Christmas Eve and Christmas Day services subsides, a time of sacred leisure seems fitting and much needed. As someone who came to the religious life as an activist, "doing" is my tendency. I need regular reminders, liturgical reminders, to take breaks, otherwise I may just keep going.

In searching for ways out of my own busyness, I came across the Greek concepts of time—the chronological time of *kronos* and open-ended *kairos* time. God's time and moment of revelation does not follow our timeline based on hours, days, or even years. It is expansive, continuous, and instantaneous all at once. Our *kronos*-heavy culture will always resist moving into *kairos* time, but perhaps for the twelve days of Christmastide we can intentionally enter into a time warp and just be still, and know that God is God. Perhaps we can receive the gift of Christ entering into the world and abiding with us, and prepare ourselves through physical rest and spiritual nourishment for the tough work of ministry that will always be there for us.

> *[Jesus] said to the apostles,*
> *"Come away to a deserted place*
> *all by yourselves and rest a while."*
> *For many were coming and going,*
> *and they had no leisure even to eat.*

— Mark 6:31

A Promise Kept

Go, tell it on the mountain,
over the hills and everywhere;
go, tell it on the mountain,
that Jesus Christ is born.
Down in a lowly manger the humble Christ
was born,
and God sent us salvation that blessed
Christmas morn.

— *Go, Tell It on the Mountain*
Nineteeth-century African American Spiritual

Christmas creates joyful sentiments. But what about our salvation—what do we make of it during Christmastide? Salvation, from the Greek *soteria*, means more than the promise of life eternal. It means health, deliverance, redemption, and wholeness. Soteria was the Greek goddess of safety and deliverance from harm; there was also Soter, her male counterpart. In ancient Greece, deliverance and safety were sought out in daily life in physical, mental, and spiritual form. For the Hebrew people, the notion of redemption (*ge'ulah*) comes from a messiah, a political ruler who would reign in a peaceful kingdom after years of strife.

Our tradition has inherited these Hebrew and Greco-Roman influences and reformulated them over two thousand years. Salvation, from a personal experience to the salvation of a people, has long been seen as something to be attained in the physical life on earth, even while believing in the resurrection of souls after death.

As such, the promised land was a real place as well as an ongoing reality to the Israelites—a land flowing with milk and honey. It was the life's mission of their people, generation after generation, to follow God's promise and get there. Even when they did get there, and things didn't always go as planned, the work of redemption continued. Martin Luther King Jr. understood this reality well when he used the reference in the last speech he gave before he was assassinated:

> *And He's allowed me to go up to the mountain. And I've looked over. And I've seen the promised land. I may not get*

there with you. But I want you to know
tonight that we, as a people, will get to the
promised land.

— "I've Been to the Mountaintop,"
April 3, 1968, Memphis, Tennessee

Such is the image of salvation that I have when I hear renditions of "Go, Tell It on the Mountain." The Christ Child, and his life's work, is about getting us to the promised land. This salvation is a total liberation from any form of bondage—it is freedom from social oppression, it is spiritual and emotional solace from the hatred of others, spiritual liberty from our own perceived limitations, a total affirmation of our God-given right to exist and thrive as God's beloved. This is reason to rejoice.

This Christmas, may we relish in our total salvation that comes to us through Christ, here for the taking and sharing as we speak.

Indeed, I know their sufferings,
and I have come down to deliver them
from the Egyptians,
and to bring them up out of that land
to a good and broad land,
a land flowing with milk and honey.

— Exodus 3:7b-8a

New Year's Eve

This night of wonder, night of joy
was born the Christ, our Brother;
he comes, not mighty to destroy,
to bid us love each other.

— Taken from *Break Forth, O Pure Celestial Light* *
Fred Pratt Green (1903-2000)

The lyrics of the popular ballad "What Are You Doing New Year's Eve," written in the 1940s, express the sentiment of the evening: "Wonder whose arms will hold you good and tight when it's exactly twelve o'clock that night, welcoming in the New Year..." The singer takes a chance in asking out a special person for New Year's Eve. Quite a bold move! But the sentiment is telling—we don't want to be alone on New Year's Eve. This is the night, for a large sector of the

---

population, that people are out somewhere—night clubs, restaurants, and public squares are filled with people—and many gather outside to watch the sky for fireworks to ring in the New Year. If people are not out, then they are probably celebrating with friends and family at someone's home. People want to be intimate, in community, on this night. It is the world's collective night of wonder and joy.

New Year's Eve, beneath the fancy attire, glasses of champagne, and dancing late into the night, shares some of the Christmas message. It is about joy and hope for the world, out with old habits that cause us harm, and in with the new ways that will restore and renew our life. It is a time to recall the year's feats, challenges, and victories, and to imagine what comes next. The recent celebration of Christ's birth, with all its newness and hope for weary souls, is a perfect predecessor to the New Year's celebrations.

We move quickly from Christmas to New Year's Day, and our lives follow this pattern of moving from one major event to another. Through this journey, we are designed for companionship and community. As companions on the journey, we can support each other's life goals and commitments made anew on New Year's Eve. Just as on that night when Christ was born, God is fully present and calls us to love each other. Even on New Year's Eve, in the midst of the night's revelry, there is another chance to enjoy a night of God's wonder, and share and count our blessings.

For you were called to freedom,
brothers and sisters;
only do not use your freedom as
an opportunity for self-indulgence,
but through love become slaves to one another.
For the whole law is summed up
in a single commandment,
"You shall love your neighbor as yourself."

— Galatians 5:13-14

New Year's Day:
Feast of the Holy Name of
Our Lord Jesus Christ

Jesus! Name of priceless worth
to the fallen of the earth,
for the promise that it gave,
"Jesus shall his people save."

— *Jesus, Name of Wondrous Love*
William Walsham How (1823-1897)

Jesus in Hebrew means *the Lord saves* or *God helps*, and Christ means *the anointed one* (the Messiah). Theologian Karl Barth notes that Jesus' name was probably Jesus *the* Christ. One was his name, and the other, his office. Jesus' name implies that he has come with a divine mission of salvation. Jesus is the bridge between two worlds—his Jewish-Galilean roots and traditions and the Greco-Roman culture and geography where his ministry would take greater hold. In Jesus Christ there is Jesus as both *person* and *work*. Through Jesus the person, God entered the world in human form; and through Jesus, God's salvific work will be done. As Barth puts it, Jesus is the "*God helps*, because he is chosen for the work and office of the Christ, the prophetic, priestly, and kingly Servant of God" (*Dogmatics in Outline*, New York: Harper & Row, 1959, 73-74).

The Feast of the Holy Name is a recognition of Jesus Christ in his fullness, as person and work. As person, Jesus will grow into full human stature and begin his ministry on the earth. He will be born in Bethlehem and will die in Jerusalem. He will travel throughout Judea, an itinerant preacher and teacher. He will recruit a team of disciples to follow him and learn the path to God. As work, Jesus will heal the sick, raise the dead, and perform other signs; he will die for preaching and teaching and healing the way that he does relentlessly; he will resurrect and reappear to his disciples. Most of all, when he embodies his fullness of person and work, his name implies a total, holy love—a love born out of God's desire to reach human souls at a profound level.

Jesus is born out of this love, heals out of this love, and speaks truth and justice out of this love. Ultimately, Jesus goes to the cross out of this love, not because he had to die, but because his love was too great for us to handle. As we meditate on Jesus' holy name and we make plans and resolutions for the New Year, may we be co-collaborators in Jesus' mission as person and work, rooted in love.

Eternal Father, you gave to your incarnate Son the holy name of Jesus to be the sign of our salvation: Plant in every heart, we pray, the love of him who is the Savior of the world, our Lord Jesus Christ. Amen.

— Collect for the Holy Name,
The Book of Common Prayer, p. 213

Swim in the Joy of the Season

Just look at how the fish
swim with delight in the river.
Look at how they swim with joy
      at the sight of God's birth.
They swim, swim,
      and then swim some more,
those fish in the river
in seeing the Savior born.

— *Los Peces en el Rio,*
Traditional Song

This song comes from Spain, and is one of the many *villancicos*, traditional Spanish songs, that are sung to commemorate the Christmas season. The lyrics may sound strange, but they have their origins in the region where the song was written.

As the story goes, the Virgin Mary has just given birth, and she is busy doing chores: washing diapers and then bathing in the local river. While she seems temporarily inattentive to her newborn, the Christ Child, because she is so focused on her bath, the fish in the river are swimming joyfully. The chorus above describes how the fish are swimming with delight because they are excited about the birth of the Christ Child.

In many of the traditional Christmas hymns, the focus is on the angels and on the heavens singing praises to God, honoring the nativity of Jesus. This song follows this tradition, but focuses on the fact that all of God's creation, even the animals, are marveling at Christ's birth. This is a very popular song of the season in Latin American communities.

In my church, this song begins slowly in the first verse, and picks up tempo with each verse until at the end it's sung so fast that it's hard to sing along! This is part of the playfulness of the song, and it also gives the impression of the fish swimming ever so quickly and excitedly in the river. People in the congregation begin to clap along, trying to keep up with the beat, and some even dance. Parents chuckle and kids laugh out loud. This song picks up on the fiesta of the Christmas Eve *Posada* and carries it into

Christmastide. In continuing the *Posada* tradition of a living, embodied faith, parishioners become like the fish, God's creation in awe and joy of the infant Christ.

How might you add some spiritual playfulness to your Christmas to-do list? What kinds of things can you do at home, as a family, or at church to bask in the joy of the season?

Make a joyful noise to the LORD,
all the earth;
break forth into joyous song
and sing praises.

— Psalm 98:4

Remember Our Roots

For he is our childhood's pattern,
day by day like us he grew;
he was little, weak and helpless,
tears and smiles like us he knew.
And he feeleth for our sadness,
and he shareth in our gladness.

—*Once in David's Royal City*
Cecil Frances Alexander (1818-1895)

This hymn appeals to me because it speaks to the humanness of Jesus. While I understand why many of the traditional hymns of the season use words that refer to Jesus in triumphant, regal terms, I have a hard time with it. I can spiritually accept the notion that Jesus was both human and divine, without having to understand it analytically. But even so, the place I turn to for comfort, when I call on Jesus, is his deep humanity. And his deep humanity began with the conditions under which he entered this world. For this, I turn to what my high school English teacher called the "5 W's plus H" of the matter: the who/what/where/when/why/how of Jesus—Jesus, born to Mary, in a manger in Bethlehem, late at night, to redeem humanity, through God's love. In knowing Jesus at this most intimate, human level, I can identify with him, and then feel that he can identify with me. How it actually happened is God's love and mystery.

It is significant that Jesus entered the world as an infant, and this hymn points to that significance. Jesus had to experience life as a fully human being with a divine plan. He had to be a toddler; he had to go where his parents went and do as his parents said; he had to grow into adulthood, to get to the point where he was fully prepared for his life's call. In his ministry, depending on which gospel you read, he showed his human moments: frustration and righteous indignation, exhaustion, and even desperation. He wept. Most of all, he showed his deep love for people and his commitment to their transformation. He wasn't just "playing human"—he *was* human and he couldn't help it.

For me, having this Jesus grounded in true life experience makes his divinity possible and accessible to me as his follower. It gives me the courage to follow his example, to draw from my own innate spiritual power that also comes from God. During Christmas, Jesus calls on us to remember his roots, remember our own, and to get to the business of making the kingdom real.

> *Let the same mind be in you*
> *that was in Christ Jesus, who,*
> *though he was in the form of God,*
> *did not regard equality with God*
> *as something to be exploited,*
> *but emptied himself,*
> *taking the form of a slave,*
> *being born in human likeness.*

— Philippians 2:5-7

Participate in Faith

Rise up, shepherd, and follow;
it will lead to the place
where the Christ was born;
rise up, shepherd, and follow;
follow the Star to Bethlehem.

—*Rise Up, Shepherd, and Follow*
Traditional Spiritual

A few years ago, when our second daughter was just three months old, my wife and I were asked by our church to participate in an important annual tradition of the season—the Christmas pageant. And not just as any participants—but as Mary and Joseph, with our daughter playing baby Jesus! And with that, our daughter started her acting career.

In all seriousness, the best part of taking part in the pageant was being a participant observer. That year, Mary and Joseph didn't have any lines, and the Christmas story was enacted entirely through the voice and perspective of the shepherds of Luke's Gospel account. The only speakers were a narrator, the shepherds, and the angel announcing Jesus' birth. As the holy family, my wife and I were sitting at the front of the church, listening to the dialogue taking place; we laid "baby Jesus" in the makeshift crib in front of us, hoping there would be no tears!

Listening to the entire narrative from the shepherds' point of view was amazing. The story took the congregation through the initial fear of the shepherds, to their amazement at the news received from the angel, to the joy and peace that they felt once they found the Christ Child, and to the gusto with which they began spreading the good news. How was it, they wondered, that God would come to them—lowly shepherds—as the first people to receive the good news of Christ's birth and to witness the heavenly band of angels singing God's praises!

The shepherds were really the first believers of the living Christ (aside from Mary and Joseph), and they were ecstatic evangelizers. The shepherds' words and actions gave great comfort to Mary, as she meditated on the blessed work that God had given her to do and on the healing and wholeness that Jesus would bring to people throughout the lands.

Participating in the pageant as a silent actor helped me better appreciate the important role that the shepherds played in the Christmas story and in beginning to spread the hope and joy of the Christ Child. May we approach our faith with the same love and amazement of the shepherds, and spread the joy!

The shepherds returned,
glorifying and praising God
for all they had heard and seen,
as it had been told them.

— Luke 2:20

Twelfth Night

Now to the Lord sing praises,
all you within this place,
and with true love and brotherhood
each other now embrace.

—*God Rest You Merry Gentleman*
Traditional Carol, Eighteenth Century

In the Twelve Days of Christmas, from Christmas Day to Epiphany, tonight is the Twelfth Night. Liturgically and traditionally, the entire twelve days were an unceasing time of celebrating the joy of Christ's coming. Socially, in the Middle Ages of Europe, this was the time for people to be with their families and rest from their labors. The Vigil of Twelfth Night was also a time of revelry and street festivals such as the Feast of Fools, similar to *Mardi Gras* for Lent, where the theological themes of Christmas entered into the public square. Based on the humble conditions under which the divine became human—as a baby born in a manger to a family living on the margins—people looked at this as a time of things being turned upside-down. People swapped and took on unlikely identities, and mimicked the religious and political structures of the day. Many of the participants were young people, poor people, and other groups on the social margins. The medieval church's usual response was to sharply condemn the activities and distance itself as much as possible, preferring to uphold the dominant group or tradition.

People, and especially those on the margins, have always needed an outlet to release and channel their repressed or excluded emotions, frustrations, dreams, and desires. Today, festivals or rituals like *Mardi Gras, Carnaval* in Brazil, *Las Posadas*, and others continue, but how often have we as the church failed to recognize the message beneath the revelry? Have we written off youth, ethnic groups, the LGBT community, single parents, or any other group on the margins, holding fast to traditions that represent and reflect only a portion of our population?

The Twelve Days of Christmas—that period of unbroken joy—and in particular the Twelfth Night is a time where we can lift up the experiences, traditions, and voices of our diverse faith community, to sing the Lord's praises in many different ways, and somehow hold it all together. What if we celebrated the season using Christ's marginal origins as the true starting point, or held our own modern-day Feast of Fools? With this Christ of the manger at our center, we would surely seek to broaden our view and reach, and invite marginalized voices and traditions into our faith communities.

So I commend enjoyment,
for there is nothing better for people
under the sun
than to eat, and drink, and enjoy themselves,
for this will go with them in their toil
through the days of life
that God gives them
under the sun.

— Ecclesiastes 8:15

January 6

The Epiphany:
Feast of the Three Kings

The star guided them on the way,
stopping at the manger.
They were filled with joy
to find the Child King.

— *Los Tres Reyes Magos*
Traditional (Author's translation)

The beginning processional at my church, on this day, looks a little different than usual. Gaspar, Melchior, and Balthasar—the Three Kings (Wise Men) from the East—have joined the procession, and follow the star to Bethlehem, in search of the infant Jesus. They come decked out in their royal attire and crowns, bearing gifts for the newborn king. Together, the entire congregation, guided by the Three Kings, sing a lively song that speaks of their journey. A festive mood is in the air. At the end of the service, the Three Kings remain and give the children little treats.

As a Mexican American, I grew up learning and maintaining some cultural traditions from my background and losing others. I didn't grow up celebrating the Feast of Three Kings. We didn't have Santa Claus either, and usually opened presents by the Christmas tree at midnight of Christmas Eve. In experiencing Three Kings' Day in recent years at my church, I wish my family had celebrated it! In many Latino/a families and regions, the *Fiesta de los Tres Reyes* is the highly anticipated culmination of the Christmas season, especially for children. The tradition came from Spain to the Americas during the colonial period, and has taken on a life of its own throughout Latin America.

Some of the customs parallel the Santa Claus tradition of gift-giving. In Puerto Rico, children collect grass or hay on the eve of Three Kings' Day, and place it in a box under or by their beds. In the evening, the Three Kings "arrive," looking for the infant Jesus, their horses stop to eat, and the Kings leave presents in the boxes. In Mexico, children leave their shoes out instead of boxes, sometimes with a little note to the Three Kings, and the Kings leave little treats or presents in their shoes. With the growing popularity of

Santa Claus, many families have split their gift-giving between Christmas and Three Kings' Day.

With our focus on moving into the Epiphany season, we often lose a little bit of the Three Kings' traditions. Thankfully, in many Episcopal churches with Latino/a congregations the tradition is being recovered, so that all may enjoy and take part.

When they saw that the star had stopped,
they were overwhelmed with joy.
On entering the house,
they saw the child with Mary his mother;
and they knelt down and paid him homage.

— Matthew 2:10-11

How To Use This Book

for

Advent 2012 and Beyond

Advent can begin as early as November 27 and as late as December 3, depending on what day of the week Christmas will fall.

Cheer Our Spirits, Make Safe the Way is a daily devotional structured for Advent 2012 to Epiphany 2013, where Advent begins on December 2, but includes additional readings so you can pray with this book year after year.

Because the meditations in this book are based on hymns and carols rather than the Scripture for the day, they can be read in any order. For Advent 2012, simply read through the book as it is. For years in which Advent does not begin on December 2, you will need to make some modifications between December 6 and 16.

Begin reading the meditations in order, but switch to the feast day readings for December 6 and 12, the Gaudete Sunday Reading for the Third Sunday of Advent, and fill in with readings from the Additional Meditations as needed, until you begin the *Las Posadas* readings on December 16. These step-by-step directions will guide you:

- Begin with the First Sunday of Advent and continue reading in order until December 6.

- On December 6, read the meditation for the Feast of Saint Nicholas (p. 19).

- On December 7 continue on with the reading for the day (e.g., Second Wednesday in Advent) until December 12. Use one of the Additional Meditations if needed (p. 117-131).

- On December 12, read the meditation for the Feast of the *Virgen de Guadalupe* (p. 37).

- On December 13, continue on with the reading for the day. Use one of the Additional Meditations if needed (p. 117-131).

- If the Third Sunday of Advent comes before December 16, read the *Gaudete* or Rose Sunday meditation (p. 129) on that day. The next day continue on with a reading of your choice from the Additional Meditations (p. 117-131).

- On December 16, read the meditation for the First Night of *Las Posadas* (p. 49). From this day on, all the readings have a calendar date; please continue reading in order through Epiphany, January 6.

We hope you will, as author Francisco J. García says, be drawn in song and prayer "into the journey and joy of the season," from Advent to Epiphany.

— *The Editors of Forward Movement*

Keep on the Path

Make ye straight what long was crooked,
make the rougher places plain;
let your hearts be true and humble,
as befits his holy reign.

— *Comfort, Comfort Ye My People*
Johann G. Olearius (1611-1684)

Our culture covets instant gratification. Just think of all the popular sayings such as "have your cake and eat it too," or "taking the easy way out." Given this, we might look to the words of this hymn wanting the crooked road to be straightened and the rough places made plain, in our time. We want life to be refined, free of worries and struggle. But this is not the way of a life of faith, nor the Advent message.

Adolescence is often the time when we most strongly experience this impatient angst, expressed in the countless songs and stories of each generation. Regardless of class, race, gender, ethnicity, or other differences, all youth face a longing desire to grow up. As a first generation born in the United States child, with parents who were learning a new language, new laws, educational systems, and social norms, I grew up in an incredibly strict household. I assumed this was normal until I spoke with friends and realized how much more lax their parents were. I couldn't spend the night at a friend's house, "because you have your own bed to sleep in." I couldn't wear baggy pants—"You might get confused with a *cholo* (gang member)." The list goes on. While I could have rebelled tremendously (and on many occasions wanted to), I also feared the consequences—not only of my parents' discipline, but also that I might do something to ruin my future. I knew that in the long run, my parents were looking out for me. So I rebelled creatively, finding avenues for participation in band and sports. I held on to the hope that if I did well in my studies, I would have greater independence in college. This proved true; struggling creatively through my adolescent years paid off.

When traveling on winding roads, it's hard to see where we are going. If the road is rough, our experience is not so pleasant. Advent is a good time to humbly ask, as we await Christ, for our bumpy and winding paths to be eased. God's reign is one of truth, humility, and clarity, where the path is made increasingly more known to us as we travel along it. The bumps alert us that something is in process, that the rough places are struggling to make themselves plain. We may never get to a completely straight path, but we aspire to and pray for it.

You need to persevere,
so that when you have done the will of God,
you may receive what was promised.

— Hebrews 10:36

The Oneness
of Death and Life

I'm just a poor wayfaring stranger,
I'm traveling through this world below;
There is no sickness, toil, nor danger,
in that bright world to which I go.
I'll soon be free from every trial,
this form will rest beneath the sod;
I'll drop the cross of self-denial,
and enter in my home with God.

— *Wayfaring Stranger*
Traditional American Folksong

While completing my chaplaincy internship at a local hospital, I met a lot of families that were dealing with the passing of their loved ones. Some of the most powerful moments that I spent in the last year occurred in the small, dizzying atmosphere of the critical care units of the hospital, a place of intimate, sacred transition from the physical life to the next life.

The process of shepherding the dying and their family members along was like none other. In one of my most intense encounters,

I recall splitting my time between two families who were forced to make end-of-life decisions under stressful conditions. While there were tense moments, as family members disagreed over whether or not to withdraw artificial life support, the breakthroughs came during the ad hoc prayer services that I facilitated according to their wishes. As part of these services at the bedside of their loved one, family members took turns sharing their most present memory of that person—whatever it might be—before withdrawing life support. In one room, there were close to twenty family members present, each one sharing a story. It took some time, but it was important, holy time, and the hospital staff were generous with the time and space. In both cases, family members who had been feuding made peace when they affirmed their mutual love for their family member who was soon to cross over, and reaffirmed that all of life's moments are sacred.

The song "Wayfaring Stranger" might not be considered a traditional Advent hymn by many, but it very much fits the mold. It captures the entire journey of the soul—modeled by Jesus' birth, life, death, resurrection, and ascension—that begins with God, travels the earth for some time in bodily form, and then returns to God. It acknowledges the difficulty often found in life circumstances, and the hope of the next life. We can find hope in the peace of the next life during Advent, but more importantly, rejoice that we can achieve a sort of freedom—through embodying love—in the way we approach the trials of *this* life.

> *If you would indeed behold the spirit of death,*
> *open your heart wide unto the body of life.*
> *For life and death are one,*
> *even as the river and the sea are one.*

—Kahlil Gibran, "On Death," in *The Prophet*

Known and Protected

O Lord, I know you are near,
*   standing always at my side.*
You guard me from the foe,
*   and you lead me in ways everlasting.*
Lord, you have searched my heart,
*   and you know when I sit*
*   and when I stand.*
Your hand is upon me protecting me from death,
*   keeping me from harm.*

— *You Are Near* *
Daniel L. Schutte (1947-   )

Recently, after final exam week in seminary, my wife took me to get a massage. It had been years since I'd had one, and it was much needed, because I had just completed the busiest and most challenging semester of my seminary studies. This particular massage practice focused on reflexology, or finding the pressure points that connect with the nervous system on key areas—head, hands, feet, and back—to relieve tension in those areas and ultimately to achieve a form of homeostasis or balance in the body. My back was in a thousand knots, my brain was like mush, and my eyes were bleary.

As the masseuse made each round of pressure movements on my head, hands, and feet, I started thinking about the roles that each of these areas of our bodies play in our life. The head, our nerve and communication center, causes us to do the things we do and say the things we say. Our hands reflect the work that we do and our ability to either embrace and greet others or to make a fist and push others away. With our feet, we take steps and walk along the paths we choose in life.

I also reflected on how I might be a better steward of my entire body and spirit. This brings me to today's hymn that calls on God, knowing that God is near. God knows our heart, but do we know our heart? God knows where and when we sit and stand. Do we know our whole selves, body and soul? Do we recognize how our bodies reflect the tensions of our lives, and how our minds and spirits are worn down by the burdens we carry?

The Lord is near, and comes nearer when we pay attention to our selves, the stressors in our lives, and our physical and emotional "reflexes"—the things that we do or say out of habit or addiction that cause us and others harm. The Lord comes nearer when we search our own hearts, minds, and bodies, to better connect with God's presence within us.

Comfort and heal all those who suffer in body, mind, or spirit; give them courage and hope in their troubles, and bring them the joy of your salvation.

— from the Prayers of the People,
The Book of Common Prayer, p. 389

Hear Us, O Lord

Creator of the stars of night,
thy people's everlasting light,
Jesus, Redeemer, save us all,
and hear thy servants when they call.

— *Creator of the Stars of Night*
Ninth Century, from the Latin;
translated by John Mason Neale

How do we know that Jesus is hearing us? Some of us have structured time each day that we spend in prayer; others of us pray whenever we can find moments alone—in the car, in the shower, when we lay down for the night. But how can we be sure that the prayers are being heard, received? For this, we need to be able to hear God as well. For this, we need to view prayer as an ongoing encounter and conversation with God, as a relationship that needs developing just like a relationship with a person. Calling out to God is part of a dynamic, reciprocal process of engagement, in which we also let ourselves be called by God. This is the ongoing work of individual or group discernment.

In my personal life of prayer, I'm weary of asking God for very specific "things" or "responses" to my life. But what I do ask for consistently is for God to make me open to the way of Jesus in my life and in the world; that I may be open to see where God is working in the world and how I might join that effort. I ask God to help me live into whatever situation or challenge is before me, and to help guide my words and actions so they might reflect God's love, justice, and compassion.

The prayer life is a cycle of praying, waiting, and listening; acting on the nudges that we feel, see, or hear; and then back again to praying, waiting, and listening. It's not a linear process, but more of a spiral of ongoing revelation. God equips us for this life's work, granting us with free will of thought and action. This is probably God's most precious gift to us. It means that God knows that we will err, yet still God trusts us.

With the coming of Christ, our mission is made even more clear. We have his way of life, ministry, and prayer as our guide. And we also have our assignment: as the body of Christ in the world, we must make our life a living prayer, where we are constantly searching and acting, trusting that God hears us when we call, and trusting that we are called.

> *My child, if you accept my words*
> *and treasure up my commandments*
> *within you,*
> *making your ear attentive to wisdom*
> *and inclining your heart to*
> *understanding;*
> *if you indeed cry out for insight,*
> *and raise your voice for understanding;*
> *if you seek it like silver, and*
> *search for it as for hidden treasures—*
> *then you will understand*
> *the fear of the Lord*
> *and find the knowledge of God.*

— Proverbs 2:1-5

Gaudete or Rose Sunday

While we walk the pilgrim pathway,
clouds will overspread the sky;
but when trav'ling days are over,
not a shadow, not a sigh.
When we all get to heaven,
what a day of rejoicing that will be!
When we all see Jesus,
we'll sing and shout the victory!

— *When We All Get to Heaven*
Eliza Edmunds Hewitt (1851-1920)

Many Christians celebrate this third Sunday of Advent as *Gaudete* (from the Latin word for "rejoice") or Rose Sunday, the day that we light the pink candle in the Advent wreath along with two violet ones, symbolizing the light that is emerging in the darkness as we approach the birth of Christ. It is also a time when we can ease our focus of examination and experience the joy of the season, in anticipation of what is to come.

The Advent journey continues, and we read and meditate on a number of scriptures to mark this place in the season—Isaiah, John, Luke. One scripture that receives a considerable amount of attention is the Magnificat, or the Song of Mary. The pilgrim pathway that we embark on during Advent really starts with Mary's call. In this song, Mary proclaims: "My soul magnifies the Lord, and my spirit rejoices in God my Savior, for he has looked with favor on the lowliness of his servant" (Luke 1:46-47). Mary, the lowly servant girl, marvels at God claiming her to do holy work.

But hold on! In the Latino/a religious tradition, Mary is not remembered as a docile, humble servant girl, but as a brave young woman who claims and proclaims God's blessing for her and her people, especially the poor and marginalized. It is this song that gives Mary the *chutzpah* (or *animo*, in the Spanish sense) to carry the divine child and to make the difficult physical journey with Joseph to Bethlehem. Mary's song is a song of joy, but it is a joy rooted in a bit of subversion, in agreeing to join God's campaign to upset the social order that has created a system of unequal souls. Mary's selection shows God's plan—that all souls are created equal before God—and Mary accepts the call to make the case. She prepares us for the rejoicing that we will all feel when we see Jesus, the Christ Child. When we get there, we'll pick up Mary's song and shout the victory of God's presence among us.

Are you ready to sing Mary's song this Advent?

> *Rejoice always, pray without ceasing,*
> *give thanks in all circumstances;*
> *for this is the will of God*
> *in Christ Jesus for you.*
> *Do not quench the Spirit.*
> *Do not despise the words of prophets,*
> *but test everything; hold fast to what is good;*
> *abstain from every form of evil.*

— 1 Thessalonians 5:16-22

About the Author

Francisco J. García, Jr., is a Master of Divinity student at the Episcopal Theological School at Claremont (Bloy House) and the Claremont School of Theology in Southern California, and a Candidate for the Priesthood in the Episcopal Diocese of Los Angeles. He is active in peace and justice, pastoral, and multicultural ministries at his home parish, All Saints Church in Pasadena. Francisco receives joy and strength for the journey from his wife and his two young daughters.

García is a contributor to Forward Movement's *Changing Diapers, Changing Lives: Reflections for New Parents* and is the author of the September 2012 issue of *Forward Day by Day*.

Hymns and Resources

The words of the hymns used in this booklet are in the public domain, unless otherwise noted.

There are often multiple versions of the non-copyrighted compositions, which you can find in numerous print publications and online, including:

Flor y Canto Hymnal
Portland, OR: OCP Publications, 2001

The Hymnal 1982
New York: Church Publishing, Inc., 1985

Lift Every Voice and Sing II:
    An African American Hymnal
New York: Church Publishing, Inc., 1993

Oremus at www.oremus.org

Voices Found: Women in the Church's Song
New York: Church Publishing, Inc., 2003

For more information about *Las Posadas*:

Mestizo Worship: A Pastoral Approach to Liturgical Ministry, by Virgilio P. Elizondo and Timothy Matovina. Collegeville, MN: Liturgical Press, 1998

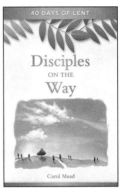